GENESIS 101

CONCLUSION

GENESIS 101

The Metaphysical Cosmology in the Process of Creation

**Understanding Your Role as the
Co-creator of Your Life**

Dr. Ronald P. Rozzi, MsD, RHy

GENESIS 101: THE METAPHYSICAL COSMOLOGY IN THE PROCESS OF CREATION

This book is written to provide information and motivation to readers. Its purpose is not to render any type of psychological, legal, or professional advice of any kind. The content is the sole opinion and expression of the author, and not necessarily that of the publisher.

Copyright © 2019 by Dr. Ronald P. Rozzi Ms.D., RHy.

All rights reserved. No part of this book may be reproduced, transmitted, or distributed in any form by any means, including, but not limited to, recording, photocopying, or taking screenshots of parts of the book, without prior written permission from the author or the publisher. Brief quotations for noncommercial purposes, such as book reviews, permitted by Fair Use of the U.S. Copyright Law, are allowed without written permissions, as long as such quotations do not cause damage to the book's commercial value. For permissions, write to the publisher, whose address is stated below.

Scripture quotations marked KJV are from the Holy Bible, King James Version (Authorized Version). First published in 1611. Quoted from the KJV Classic Reference Bible, copyright ©1983 by the Zondervan Corporation.

Printed in the United States of America.

ISBN   978-1-64552-148-8   (Paperback)
ISBN   978-1-64552-149-5   (Digital)

Lettra Press books may be ordered through booksellers or by contacting:

Lettra Press LLC
30 N Gould St. Ste N
Sheridan, WY 82801, USA
3035861431 | info@lettrapress.com
www.lettrapress.com

CONTENTS

Metaphysics: Beyond the Physical into the Spiritual ix
Introduction xi

Section 1: God's Work: From the World to You 1

Section 2: The Laws 15
    The Law of Attraction 17
    The Law of Cause and Effect 18
    The Law of Correspondence 19
    The Law of Belief 19
    The Law of Vibration 20
    The Law of Action (Inspired) 21
    The Law of Detachment 23
    The Law of Gratitude 24

Section 3: Roadblocks 27

Section 4: Steps 39

Section 5: Bonus Exercise 47
    Sixty-Eight Seconds 47

Section 6: Bonus Laws 51
    The Law of Perpetual Transmutation 51
    The Law of God Action 52

    The Law of Reversibility 55
    The Law of Inverse Transformations 55

Section 7: Awareness and Quantum Physics 57

Section 8: An Ending and a Beginning 61

Section 9: New Lifestyle 65

Section 10: Simplicity, Inspiration, and Empowerment 69

About the Author 73
Certifications 75
Acknowledgments 79
Resources 81

This book is dedicated in the memory of my first wife, Ann Goodwin-Rozzi. It was her early and untimely death at twenty-five that projected me into seeking answers. I needed to know about this death thing. I needed to know if she was all right. I needed to be comforted in some kind of understanding of this whole experience. Why, and for what purpose, did this happen to her after marrying me and having a three-year-old son? I dug deep for answers and found myself immersed in metaphysics and spirituality.

I found answers, one being that it was part of her life purpose. I found peace, and I found a passion. I am thankful for that blessing.

METAPHYSICS: BEYOND THE PHYSICAL INTO THE SPIRITUAL

All things are governed by universal laws, whether physical or spiritual. In everything there is order. There is a system of design by infinite intelligence. He is a being known as God and many other names. The universal laws are simply an extension of His being.

Meta means above, beyond, and behind.

Metaphysical means beyond the physical realm and into the spiritual realm. The metaphysical and physical realm are not two separate realities; they are simply different levels of the same reality.

Metaphysics is the branch of philosophy that examines the fundamental nature of all reality.

This includes the relationship between mind and matter, appearance and substance, and form and essence. To call one a metaphysician in this traditional, philosophical sense indicates nothing more than his or her interest in attempting to discover what underlines everything. In order to examine the nature of physical reality, we must do so from a level above it. Einstein said that we can never solve a problem in the same level of consciousness with which it was created. We have to advance to a higher level and deal with it powerfully.

There is an absolute science to all things spiritual.

It isn't as mysterious as it seems. It's only mysterious according to the level of awareness we have. The higher our level of awareness, the more the mystery is resolved.

Cosmology is a branch of metaphysics that deals with the nature of the universe.

INTRODUCTION

This journey you are about to embark on is laid before you with unconditional love. It represents for me a work of inspiration from spirit through me. I have been silently hounded for years now to put pen to paper and share what excites me most at this point of my life experience. I don't mind admitting that I'm a little slow at the draw, but I know without a doubt that everything in this universe is timely. I won't question the fact that had I started younger, I could have done and enjoyed more relative to sharing my passion. I'm right on time, and therefore so are you. It is my mission and purpose in this incarnation, at least at this time. I've learned not to question, only to allow what is coming forth at this time.

The paths of self-development and self-realization started for me back in the late seventies via a personal tragedy, which ultimately became a blessing and a window of growth. In my personal process of healing, I asked deep questions and was shown avenues of answers that changed the whole direction of my life. Of course, I didn't realize what was happening at the time, but I did begin to think about sharing what I was being shown with others. A part of me "sang" inside, and it felt right somehow. This was for my healing but was not to keep for myself. I literally vibrated and resonated with harmony when I thought about it. It took me quite a while to realize that this was the higher part of me calling to me and identifying itself as purpose. Since those days, many more life experiences were added to my resume on life, some good and some not so good, but all were important parts of the package of presenting this material to you.

Little by little, I involved myself with sharing what helped and excited me, or what I was compelled to share, getting deeper and deeper into the mysteries and metaphysics of the life process. All the while, I was trying to balance living and working a "normal" life. This was not easy, as you will soon see within the contents of this book. But if your desires are deep enough, your passion to express life is hot enough, and you can hear the silent voice of spirit, then it can be done. Like anything of worth, however, there is a price, and only you can determine what cost you're willing to pay.

In getting to a place where I can now get this material to you, I will admit that I learned many valuable life lessons from a variety of well-meaning and wonderful people who, through being who they were, taught and encouraged me to do the same. This book is me expressing and being … well, me. That is not only my but everyone's birthright. Enough said about that.

After over seventeen years in private practice helping hundreds of people with a variety of challenges via hypnosis, EFT, and metaphysical counseling, I looked and listened to what common denominator was in all this. It stood out like the preverbal sore thumb: it was *awareness*! Awareness of who we really are as a being, form our earliest beginning. Awareness of the power we all have as co-creators of our own lives. Awareness of the laws of life and how to use them to bring to us (or manifest) the health, peace, or success that we choose. To top it off, the awareness of how to circumvent the roadblocks we encounter once we decide it's time for change.

The laws of life are clear-cut and immutable; they have always been and always will be. The problem is that most folks, even the most well-meaning souls, don't know of them or how they work, and they unknowingly transgress them through thoughts, words, and deeds. Universal law is impartial, and doesn't recognize us personally, and so people get the corresponding negative results, otherwise known as dysfunctions, diseases, disappointments, and unhealthy patterns. Now they live in states of fear ("**f**alse **e**vidence **a**ppearing **r**eal") at some level for most of their adult lives. The keyword here for our purposes is adult. You see, 99 percent of my clients over the years have been adults. Oh, I'd see the occasional child with a loving parent or caregiver in tow, but it was the exception and not the rule. This is not to say children don't have problems, because many souls are born into some kind of negative or fear-based platform. It simply doesn't always show up in recognizable degrees until they become adults with lives of responsibility and "stuff."

Working with people of all kinds and with challenges of all kinds, I'd be able to impart upon them my passion to some degree: words of wisdom, ideas, and concepts that they really knew, but didn't know they knew. I delighted in seeing many aha moments in their eyes—subtle indications that they had figured it out and somehow got it! I could introduce to them why their lives were the way they were based on laws that they were transgressing; hopefully I did so without offence to their integrity, and always in a loving manner. Once they had this new awareness, they could better implement positive change in their own lives, on their own and without being dependent upon me. I've always worked on the premise of self-empowerment and give my people tools in addition to ideas and concepts. We are self-creating, self-healing spiritual beings that are having experiences in human bodies, which in turn can only mirror our inside worlds of emotions and beliefs. Go forward from my office to create your life now by deliberate intention rather than by default.

The more I shared this with the select few that the universe brought to my door, the more I realized and understood that mass awareness from an individual basis could ultimately change the world. Changing the world is no small task. I didn't really want to change the world. All I felt was needed was to do something that could possibly change the world of at least one person, and I knew in my heart that that one could pass it on in some fashion to another, and so on. I found my marching orders.

In order to fulfill my mission to bring this awareness into light for you, I feel it's necessary to go to the beginning of beginnings about you. Hence, Genesis 101 is presented.

This work has been put together to take you by the hand and help you to first understand that it's your duty to live your life to the fullest, because it is a gift from God, the Creator. Second, it will help you understand a little bit about the Creator from more a metaphysical rather than a religious perspective. It is not my intent to push anyone toward any particular religion or philosophy. The title of this book is Genesis 101, and so the starting point must be with God because we are dealing with life.

Next, we will look at the laws that God put into place relative to creation itself. Creation of anything follows a set process—the very process that God used to manifest the world from absolute nothingness. The physical world and our personal worlds are really quite similar, differing only in size and content. Not only must we know of and understand these laws, but we should see how each one plays a key part in creating or manifesting the things and or changes we may be seeking. We know that in order to build any building in our physical world, there are physical laws that we need to understand and adhere to so that it stands erect and doesn't crumble at the first storm. Well, in order to rebuild aspects of our lives, there are non-physical laws in place, and we need to follow them so that we too can stand erect.

Fourth, we need to look at any personal road blocks or brick walls that may be in the way of our building process. Once again, to use the analogy of building, the most important part is the foundation. If, in digging that foundation, we come across any huge rocks or tree stumps, it isn't safe to go around them, is it? We need to dig them out, or else the foundation will be uneven and weak. If we don't, then no matter what good material we build on top of it, it will not be solid and will come crashing down.

Lastly, let's tie the work up with an easy-to-understand, step-by-step application of everything we've talked about. It is my intent to make this information informative, inspiring, practical, and easy to understand for the average person who sincerely wants to make changes, or who wants to get more out of his or her life. More quality, more fun, and more adventure.

It's really about expressing our passions, isn't it? We all have them somewhere inside. We were born into this world for a reason, but so few actually get an opportunity to identify their passions, let alone express and share them. We are taught basic morals and values from birth from our parents, and we accept them usually without question. Then we move on to be schooled by institutions that have their own agendas on what is important for us to know and understand. I'm not saying that this is all bad, but it limits us from understanding the whole picture and truth of life and how it works. This material simply isn't taught to the masses like it should be from the earliest times we can comprehend as children.

Anyway, we graduate, and maybe go to a higher institution for more limited learning. Or maybe not. We get jobs, get married, have a family, and begin the process all over again with another generation that will look to us for answers. For most of us, a good life can be had, and we need to be thankful for the blessings and bounty we've enjoyed along the way. However, at some point for some of us, there is that still small voice inside that cries out very subtly at first, but over time as it's ignored, it gets louder: "What about me?" There seems to be a hole in our souls that needs recognition and nourishment.

Okay, here is the truth: there is nothing wrong with you! You are a marvelous being created in the likeness and image of an all-encompassing, loving God. He has bestowed upon you the gift of life, and that includes talents, abilities, and most important, an agenda to be carried into the realm of the physical by the soul, in order for that soul to experience various states of being. There are no accidents or mistakes; everything is divinely orchestrated according to His agenda for the purpose of your evolution and the evolution of mankind. You have free will to choose to express your life to the fullest, or simply to accept your lot and not grab for the gusto of life. Neither is wrong, but one sure sounds more fun. God doesn't put things in our world for us to not have or enjoy them. He is expressed through you, my friend. You are doing God, yourself, and the world an injustice by not expanding. If I were to give you a gift wrapped with a pretty bow, would you let it sit on your desk and stare at it unopened, or would you want to see what was inside?

Let's take off the blinders, take a walk into what may have been unknown to you, and make it known. Feel the excitement, feel the growth, and most important feel the power. After all, something led you here.

SECTION 1

God's Work: From the World to You

Genesis is a noun related to the Greek word *gignesthai*, which means to be born, begin, start, commence, or open.

There's something optimistic about these words, whether they refer to the dawn of a new day, the birth of a child, the prelude of a symphony, or the first miles of a family vacation. Free of problems and full of promise, beginnings stir hope and imaginative visions of the future.

The word *genesis* means beginnings or origins. It unfolds the record of the beginning of the world, human history, family, civilization, and salvation. As the book of beginnings, Genesis sets the stage for the entire Bible. It reveals the person and nature of God, the value and dignity of human beings, the tragedy and consequences of sin, and the promise and assurance of salvation.

God—that is where Genesis begins. All at once, we see Him creating the world in a majestic display of power and purpose. The people we meet in Genesis are simple, ordinary people; yet through them, God did great things.

There is hope! No matter how dark the world's situation seems, God has a plan. No matter how insignificant or useless you feel, God loves you and wants you to experience your evolution. No matter how sinful and separated from God you think you are, His presents is available. Open your eyes and heart.

Let us upset the applecart here right from the start. I'm suggesting that you let go of whatever you think you know. Let's walk together in your unknown, or at least in what wasn't in the basic schoolbooks or self-help material you may have read. Look at your life like it's a giant iceberg in the Arctic Ocean. What you see on top is only a fraction of what's underneath. I realize that you understand there is an underneath to an iceberg, but because you can't see it, it would be nearly impossible to determine its total mass without diving into the depths.

Similarly, in your life, you know what's on top: what you look like, what's going on in your life, what you may be feeling via emotions or physical discomforts, et cetera. Your conscious memory can conjure up a good portion of your childhood memories with relative clarity. Outside of that, as you see yourself, your life may look like a narrow band of memories, emotions, and experiences—some good and some not so good.

At this point, I would venture to suppose that if you have any degree of normalcy, you've asked yourself a time or two a couple of questions. "Is this all there is? Who am I, really?" Just think about the answers your parents or educators gave you as you were growing up. Answers to questions such as, where you came from for instance. How about what you learned in health class about the process of birth? I'm willing to bet that the answers you received or what you learned from a text book never clarified the deeper mysteries of life and your part in it.

Your life must be seen from the unseen so that you can get at least a glimmer of understanding of just how absolutely magnificent and powerful you really are, knowing that you were conceived in pure love with intent and purpose from the Creator (God, Infinite Intelligence, First Cause, or whatever label you choose). You need to accept the fact that you didn't simply show up by yourself through your physical parents.

Birth has been called a miracle, and it truly is. Not only did you show up here and now, but also you have a purpose and a mission. Both are yours and yours alone to expose and live out before you leave this dimension of reality. It is sad to see folks who live out their lives in quiet desperation, not venturing out beyond their comfort zones to explore the possibilities that lie before them. So often we become wounded in our walks of life, and it causes scars that run deep and bring us to points of despair and hopelessness. It's true we are here to explore and learn, and falling down is all part of life. However—and you've heard this before—it's not the fall but the getting back up that's sometimes tough. By realizing and embracing the truth of who you really are, you will be able to not only get back up but also be wise to why you fell in the first place. With a deeper understanding of your true being, not only will your perspective of circumstances change, but you'll also understand how to make the changes you desire and gravitate to a better, more fulfilling lifestyle utilizing the unseen universal laws of creation that have always been there, waiting for you to unleash in your life. This is exciting.

I bet the vast majority of you have some kind of belief in the fact there is something greater out there that is responsible for a lot of stuff we don't understand. Personally, I don't just believe it—I *know* it, and I choose to call that something greater God. Sometimes I will refer to God with different names, but you'll know what I mean as we go along.

Life is all around us; it is a presence of energy, light, vibration consciousness, and intelligence. God is that totality, or what will be now known as universal life energy, or Source. God is the foundation and the apex of all existence. This Source is also the purest form of love that we can't even begin to imagine. Now we've got this love, this intelligence, and this consciousness that always was and always will be. It presents itself as light, energy, and vibration. May we agree, for the sake of this material making any sense to you, that God is (among many things) an energy source? It is pure consciousness that is intelligence and love personified. It is the energy source that makes up all life. God is everywhere and in all things. Let that be our accepted truth.

In order to look at your life, we have to examine life in general from its genesis. For now, we don't mean you specifically, but humans in general. In so doing, we will walk for a short bit, touching and reflecting on the very first parts of the Christian Bible relative to creation. The book of Genesis is, after all, about beginnings. Bear in mind that it is only one explanation, and there are many others whose combined teachings weave the story of truth into a complete, unified pattern. All in all, it will help us as we transition into the metaphysics of life and the self at that connection to God, the Creator of it all.

The Creator's purpose in being-ness is to express itself in form. That indicates that the starting point of all creation is the Word of God. The Word is the concept, the idea, the image, or the thought of God. It is the self-knowing mind speaking itself into manifestation. This Word begets a movement that we'll call vibration, which denominates to what we know as thought. We know thought, being the highest form of vibration, is an inner process of consciousness, but I'm getting a little ahead of myself here.

"In the beginning, God!" In the beginning was spirit or intelligence only. No manifest universe. No system of planets. No visible form. Nothing but the life principle. God the Spirit had not yet moved upon the waters. Then this All Being moved or began to create.

Here come the questions. Where did the Spirit move? Upon what did It move? Whence came Its pattern? What means or power did It employ? Through what agencies did It work? In short, out of what is the world (ourselves included) made? How did we and all physical manifestations come into being?

Let's see if we can bring this to light in the simplest way possible without taking the splendor and divinity out of it. The previous questions, correctly answered, would solve the problem of being and set us free, at least on one level. Take a deep breath, and take it slow through here.

God was all; there was nothing else but Itself. He was all-inclusive, everywhere, and infinite. This All-Spirit could not have had the impulse to move unless It was self-conscious. Therefore, God is the power that knows Itself. It is, accordingly, all knowing as well as all present. Being one and undivided, whatever It knows, it knows all over instantly. This tells us that God operates through self-knowing. It moves, and that inner movement must be one of infinite power moving upon itself, since It is all and with a definite purpose.

The Spirit then moves upon Itself and makes out of Itself all that is made. This means that what we see comes from what we don't see, through some inner intelligence at work that knows there is no power but Itself. Again, this equates to all that we recognize in form in our physical reality is actually an effect caused from a creative process by the intelligence of either humans or God. At this point, humans aren't here yet, so let's keep going.

The only possible operation of intelligence is thought, or the Word. All things were made by the Word. The Spirit speaks, and because there is nothing but the Spirit and It is all-power, it has only to speak, and it is done. "The Word was with God and the Word was God." From the

Word then comes all that appears. Each life, each manifestation is a different kind of word coming into expression. A point to remember is that the Spirit needs nothing to help It. It is self-conscious and has all the power and ability to do whatever It wishes to accomplish; It simply speaks. The Word, which is the inner activity of thought, comes first in the creative series, and all else comes from the effect of the Word on universal substance. Think of universal substance as a kind of cosmic plastic or clay that molds the form of the desired thought.

In the Christian Bible, it tells us in Genesis 1:1–25 that God spoke the Word and in six days created the heavens, which includes all the stars, galaxies, and planets, not to mention the space we're still discovering. The skies, the land masses, the separation of the land masses from the waters. All the creatures large and small that walk and crawl the land, and the birds that fly above. The trees and vegetation of all kinds to shade and feed the creatures. Then, the Spirit, in fulfilling Its expression of Itself in form with immeasurable love, created man in Its own image, male and female. He not only created man by His Word, but He gave him dominion over all the other creatures of the newly created earth. The very least that we are, according to the Bible, is verse 26. The most of what we really are is yet to come.

The impulse of the Spirit to move into creative mode, if you will, was caused by a desire to express what It feels Itself to be. Spirit wants to enjoy Itself. It sounds simple, but remember man is now manifest and is very much a part of this process. We need to start realizing the links between this God Force and man. If you wish to prove the power of Spirit in your life, don't be short-sighted and see only what's on the outside or the effects of your world. Look to the Word and recall that what you see and what you touch is an effect of the cause. Unseen law controls everything, but this law is also an effect. The law did not make itself, and neither is it intelligence or causation. Before there is law, there has to be something that acts. Law is the way it acts.

If we could but realize that humans are like God, it would follow that there is but one mind, and therefore our words must have power because the power that holds the planets in their place is the same power that flows through us. Our words, our thoughts are the activity of that one mind in our consciousness. Mind is really the collective of the God Force—the intelligence, the love, the power, the utter majesty of life itself. It is creative, plastic, and also receptive. The slightest thought makes an impression on it. Man, is connected to God and the one mind through his soul on the invisible side, and the brain on the physical side. It was the intension of God from the beginning to give man this connection to Itself, and the activity between us is orchestrated perfectly, held by universal law.

That was a lot to chew on. The bottom line here is that creation and the process of it can be looked at, studied, and debated from now to the end of time as we know it. What we need to do here is grab hold of a piece that feels true to us and that resonates within our own souls, which as was explained is a part of the Source. Find that spark and let it grow in its own time, because it will. We don't need all the definitive answers, just a slice of light to stand on so we can move to the next avenue: you.

Let's talk about the manifest man. Life has entered into you with the irresistible impulse to create. Divine intelligence has willed it so. You belong to the universe in which you live. You are one with the Creator who orchestrates this vast array of ceaseless motion, this original flow of life. You are an expression of universal consciousness. The consciousness of you is temporarily manifesting itself in individual form through your body. What you want to remember is that you in your physical body are an extension of that which is God, or whatever you choose to call It. Because you are the furthermost extension of God, then God is also experiencing that expansion because of you, through you, and with you. I remember hearing a phrase many years ago, "we are Gods in amnesia, we are Source Energy that has incarnated into Third Dimensional Existence." That really resonated with me even before I understood its true meaning.

For most of us, the idea that we are gods is a stretch, and to some I would guess it's a statement of blasphemy that has no equal. However, consider this quote, "I have said you are gods; and all of you are children of the Most High" (Ps. 82:6). Nonetheless, I will stand on the concept that we are co-creators with the Creator, endowed with all that It is. As earlier stated, because we are pure consciousness, we are here to create whatever reality we desire. The Creator has created everything in order to experience Itself through Its creations—hence co-creators seems about right.

If we can accept that divine title of co-creator, we can move along here. I would like to point out another important concept: we are all one. Look at the creative process for man and come to terms with the concept that man (the species) must then have come with the same powers and abilities of co-creator, utilizing the one mind for all aspects of our very existence. Would it not be a truth that we are all connected? In the beginning, there was only one consciousness that existed. The one consciousness decided to differentiate Itself into the many in order to experience Itself from different perspectives and points of view. We are all different versions of the same being in existence. I believe you can substantiate this truth for yourself. Let's look at a couple of examples.

Have you ever felt sorrow or empathy for another person in times of difficulty or tragedy? If you're human, I know you have. Those very feelings you experience are the results of that person's negative energy being transmitted outward into universal consciousness and then being picked up by two of your five physical senses, your eyes and your ears, which forward it to the brain. You can actually feel the person's pain. We are connected.

Next, consider this question. What is it that we all want? Really think on that. Is it perfect health? Love? Wealth and success? All of that? I'd say yes and no. Yes, because I don't think anyone in their right mind wouldn't want any of those. But no, because it's really not those, but what those bring to us in a deeper way. How about freedom? The human spirit craves freedom above all else. Why? Because freedom is where we came from. Freedom is what we are as spiritual beings, unencumbered by our physical cloaks. The higher-self lives here. I'm sure you'd agree freedom is interpreted in many ways, but to its lowest common denominator, it is who we are. Therein lies the connection to our source and to each other.

The concept of we are all one certainly doesn't negate us from also being individuals by any means. That is an important point of freedom. We seek the freedom to be who we are, and that is key. What I'm saying is that we are really individuations of the one mind, separate but a part of the whole. Much like your fingers, each is separate with a unique purpose, but they are parts of the hand, and likewise the hand to the arm, the arm to the torso, and so on—all parts of the whole. Now, this whole we're discussing has two aspects, the physical and the nonphysical. Let's look first at the physical aspect because that's what you're probably most familiar with, and you can see what it really is. It's called the brain, the epicenter to man's connection with the Source.

The first great discovery man made was that he could think. That thinking was being taken place in his head. From that thinking came ideas, and ideas spawned some kind of effect called creating. At first, this creating was for survival purposes, and then it moved on to creating comforts and so on. As man evolved slowly along in self-discovery and began to study himself physically, he learned much about his internal parts and their functions. He developed the sciences, anatomy, biology, and physiology, and he became quite proficient in the way man worked. We all learn about these things in our schools, colleges, and universities. It's a marvelous organ, this brain, and at this point in time we are still discovering new bits of information on how it works.

For our purposes, what we need to see here is that we've come to understand that the brain in man's head is now the thinker of thought, and it has also been linked to another title, called our mind. Sometimes if we think too far beyond the norm, we're out of our minds in the eyes of some folks. As funny as that sounds, there is a bit of truth to it. One really needs to step back to see a different perspective.

A clarification about the brain is in order here. The brain really isn't the thinker, because if it could think, it would keep on thinking when removed from the body. Yet without a brain, man cannot think. I prefer to think of the organ called the brain as a complex transmitter connected with the one mind, or the Source. Thinking is the activity between the one mind and the brain of man, which is really a very high, or fast, vibration. Really, the mind as we like to call it is actually a small slice of the one mind, home of consciousness and all-knowing. Through this thinking process and the laws that it falls under, we can create things in our world from nowhere to now here. We all plug into this mind automatically and use it to various degrees, and what we receive from it comes into our brains looking like electrical impulses that have effects on our bodies in the form of feelings, emotions, inspirations, and calls to action. This slice of mind that we now access has its own compartments, if you will. We call them conscious, subconscious, and superconscious. Let us remember that what we are discussing here is related to the human brain, but the larger picture is actually the life force itself upon the mind of man.

Conscious or objective mind and thought is, for all intents and purposes, your everyday life as you know it, with most of your memories as well. Subconscious or subjective mind and thought can be likened to a huge memory stick or thumb drive that has a dual purpose. One is to quietly run the working parts of your physical body, from your heartbeat to blinking to breathing to your growth process; it's activity you never have to consciously think about doing. Second, it's a storehouse of memories that you have no need to actually recall on a day-to-day basis. Keep in mind that those memories, like your conscious memories, all have feelings and emotions attached to them, so there's a lot of content here. You process your life with the five basic senses: sight, sound, smell, touch, and taste. We can add the one nonphysical sense, otherwise known as the sixth sense of intuition. Everything—and I mean everything—that your individual life force has ever come in contact with is recorded and kept in this subconscious part of the mind; basically, the history of your soul lives here. The superconscious area of mind and thought is the God Mind itself. This is literally the seventh and highest dimension of reality. Jesus the Christ, while in human form, attained this level of consciousness; there were others through time who achieved this as well. It is my belief that the agenda of human evolution is to attain this level of awareness. As it is now, we are only third-dimensional beings.

Our sciences have proved that we actually utilize nearly 100% of our brain negating the old myth that we only use around 10% of it. That's great news, right? Despite that revelation however, it may come as a surprise that man as a species has barely evolved past infancy. I feel this is because we don't yet realize our own real power. We are totally connected to the God Force here with cosmic mind and our physical brain. We've also been given total control and permission to open the throttle.

At this point, I would like to remind you of one of the objectives I have in sharing with you in this work: to reacquaint you with who you really are and how magnificent you are, so that you can move forward to make whatever changes you want in your life and understand that it is absolutely your birthright. I'm doing that by showing you the road less traveled, or looking under the covers, if you will. I ask you once again continue to suspend your doubt and read on. Take in what you can, and leave the rest for now. Evolution is slow, but it is movement nonetheless.

I would like to bring to light one more aspect of you that is connected to God, the Source. It's a part of you that isn't physical like the brain, but it is real for sure. We call it the soul. I'm sure there are aren't many people who haven't heard of the soul, but those who have more than likely haven't put much thought into what it really is. Without getting too deep here—because it can go there, believe me—I will do my best to explain it in relation to your magnificent connection to the Source. This in turn will substantiate your true power and duty to your own life.

Have you ever read about or heard personal accounts of near-death experiences (NDEs)? Whether you believe in life after death or not is irrelevant. Most stories are similar regarding what people "saw." Rising up out of the body, looking down on it, and taking in most of the surrounding scenes. Traveling quickly through a tunnel of light and into a place of serenity, peace, and total love. Possibly seeing deceased friends and relatives who have been gone for some time but who look perfect and radiant in this place. Some may even experience divine beings or angelic figures. Mostly, however, these near-death experiencers are told by a voiceless voice that it isn't their time yet, and that they need to go back to finish out their lives in what may even be a badly injured or wrecked body. They reluctantly come back, and usually their lives are totally changed as a result of this cosmic exchange. My question to you is this: What was it that experienced that? It certainly wasn't their physical selves, but they were aware of themselves as themselves. They ultimately knew they "died," or at least they thought they did because they saw the circumstances prior to rising up, yet they had no pain. Science has its version of explanation, but I can't totally buy it. Try this model on for size because it coincides with what we're talking about.

Your soul, like your mind, is a part or individuation of the universal soul, just as your mind is to the one mind. The universal soul is the tool or medium through which God expresses Itself. The purpose of the soul, or its reason for coming to the body, is to be and express who you really are. The soul yearns to know itself. Because soul is the essence of Spirit, it knows all there is to know all the time. There is nothing hidden to it, nothing unknown. Yet knowing isn't enough—the soul seeks to experience. That experience can only be gained through you becoming the sum total of all your experiences. Hence, with soul being substance, it literally becomes an impression of your physical self, complete with consciousness of itself and all the memories of your life experiences. Every human life has this soul-self connected to it at all times, until the body dies. It is this that rises upward into higher realms of consciousness, reuniting with Source energy; we like to call this heaven. I personally theorize that people who experience an NDE and feel themselves moving through this "tunnel of light" are actually experiencing moving through the remaining layers or dimensions of reality consciousness, from the third to the seventh God realm. Here, in total love, all is revealed.

As you know from physics class, energy cannot be destroyed, only transformed. Therefore, because the soul is energy within our physical selves, it lives beyond our physical death with all its "stuff" from our life experiences intact, and in time it may need to express itself yet again in form. This of course could lead us to the subject matter concerning reincarnation, which I will leave for another time. It is really an awesome concept.

Before we move on to the next section of this material, we should probably summarize a bit here. We started looking at life from its raw beginning, the Word, the effects of the Word, being the world as we know it, and ultimately man. These things are all from our Creator, the Source, God. Then we looked a little deeper at this Creator and the story of why and how It created. Even though the principles and concepts are theoretical, because that's what metaphysics is, we kept moving. To that end, I'm willing to say that if there was the slightest ring of truth in there, you felt it because your subjective soul knew it, and there was a flash of remembering. Now, once you (man) came into the picture, I needed to just give you a glance at just how powerful, special, and loved you really are because you are a "child" of the Creator. We linked you as always being a part of that all-knowing life force energy through your brain and your soul. You are never alone because you are a part of all that is.

Hopefully, by now you have a little more insight into who you really are and what powers you. We've brought a little more clarity into the invisible part of the iceberg, shoring up the foundation for you to stand on so you can claim your true selfness as a co-creator.

SECTION 2

The Laws

This section is designed to bring an awareness to you regarding the universal laws that play a part in the creation process. Individually, you should understand a little about these few laws as you proceed to take on the role of co-creator and choose to manifest changes and the desires of your heart. I'm assuming you want to get positive results here, so it's good to know what not to do—and conversely, how to harmonize with the process, thereby moving toward your goal at the same time your goal is moving toward you.

Everything in the earth is ruled by law. We are included in that everything, because the universal laws are operating in every experience of our lives no matter who we are, where we are, or what we are doing. We are all somewhat familiar with our physical laws—the law of aerodynamics, the law of gravity, the laws of nature, and the laws of electricity, to name a few. We may not necessarily know just how they work, but we know they are in play, and in most cases, we give them the respect that they are due because if we transcend them, we could get hurt. Transcending universal laws could also hurt us with a variety of negative results in our lives that affect our health and mental well-being.

God thinks. As a result of God's thought, law is set into motion, or the thought moves as law in a field of cause and effect. The universal laws are fundamental laws of mind and spirit; they are the basic principles by which life operates. These laws are not restrictive, meaning only that they were created out of love that will produce good in your life if you choose to work with them in the right way. The essence and purpose of all universal laws and the reason for their existence is to manifest the infinite love of God to all.

There are five growth benefits as you begin to understand and work with these laws. First, you will learn how to meet and resolve the problems or traumatic conditions that you face. Second, you begin to live so as to create more peace, joy, and understanding in your life, and thereby become an example for others. Third, you come to understand how, through these laws, you make or break your relationships, your career, your finances, and your life itself. Fourth, you transform yourself and your life. Fifth, your life becomes a fulfilling one because your actions will be in accord with the purpose of the universe. Living your life without some understanding of these invisible life principles is likened to driving your car and not knowing how to control it. Know this: for the most part, the universal laws are unbreakable, unchangeable principles of life that operate inevitably in all phases of your life. However, with an awareness of them you can make some different conscious choices that will alter the effects of the laws in your current life situation.

Now that we know what they are and how important they are, we can begin to focus on the ones I've picked out of the fifty-plus that I know of, which are more specific to our needs relative to manifesting change in your arena. I will list each of the eight chosen laws and their meanings, because I feel you should have an awareness of them as you explore your ability of conscious creation. Later, when we put things together in the step-by-step section for manifesting change, you should be able to see where each one comes into play.

Universal laws never fail or waver. By choosing to review the listed universal laws, you are expanding your individual awareness, which is the sole purpose of this book. Consequently, by becoming aware of and consciously aligning and harmonizing with these laws, you will begin to know, feel, and experience for yourself that indescribable divine connection that does and always has existed.

1. **The Law of Attraction:** Simply stated, the law of attraction says that we attract into our lives that upon which we place our dominant thoughts or our belief systems (which are just crystallized thoughts). In other words, if we focus predominantly on abundance, solutions, and positive outcomes, then that is exactly what we will attract back into our lives. Conversely, the opposite is true: if we focus on lack, scarcity, and inability, that will be what shows up. Because this law operates from the subjective part of the self or mind, it is impartial to how it is directed; it only acts. Earl Nightingale, author of the book Acres of Diamonds said, "We become what we think about most of the time." Therefore the law of attraction is the law by which thought correlates with its object. The Great Teacher, Jesus, says regarding this law, "Whatsoever things ye desire when ye pray, believe you receive them and ye shall have them." The keyword here is "whatsoever," not just this or that but anything that you believe. The combination of thought, emotion, and belief create an intensified vibration or frequency into the ethers and attracts additional vibration or energy of a harmonious frequency. The result is that

which you believe (think) is manifest in the physical. You are responsible. Life is not a set of random events, conditions, and circumstances that happen by fate or chance. The law of attraction delivers to you precisely what you asked it to. Change your thoughts, and you will change your world.

2. **The Law of Cause and Effect:** This law closely resembles the law of attraction. Some scholars of metaphysics claim it is the same, but let's take a closer look. The law of cause and effect is also known as the great basic universal law, and also the law of karma. Karma, as you may or may not know, is simply the result of an action, be it physical or mental. This law states that every cause has an effect, and every effect is the cause of something else. Every effect in your life must have a corresponding cause. Nothing happens by chance outside of the universal laws; every action has a reaction or consequence. "We reap what we sow." Ralph Waldo Emerson said of the law of cause and effect, "It is the law of laws." Every human thought, word, and deed is a cause that sets off a wave of energy throughout the universe, which in turn creates the effect, whether desirable or undesirable. The law states that the effect must come to physical manifestation, be it in our bodies or the outside world. Remember, it's not just what we do but how we think, because as we already know, thought is creative. We must be aware and mindful that this law is always operating. It's important that you learn to gain control of your thoughts and weed them out so that you are utilizing the law of cause and effect to produce the results that you want, and not that which you don't want. Becoming familiar with this, as well as the other universal laws, is a huge first step in learning to become a purposeful and conscious creator of circumstance rather than a victim of circumstance.

3. **The Law of Correspondence:** This law tells us that our outer world is nothing more than a reflection of what's going on inside us. If our outer reality is unhappy, chaotic, or unfulfilling, it is a direct result of what's happening inside us. If we have a low self-esteem, feel badly about ourselves, or constantly feel anger, hatred, or loathing, then our outer world will be a place of turmoil. The sad thing is that it becomes a self-perpetuating situation. We feel badly about ourselves, which has a direct impact on our reality. In order to escape from this treadmill, it is critical to shift our paradigm. As within, so without; as above, so below. Nothing in our outer lives can change without first making changes on the inside. In fact, the basis for all self-help is change from the inside out! It does not matter one bit what we attempt to change on the outside, if we haven't done the work to change on the inside. Our reality will continue to evolve so that it is a reflection of our inner beliefs. It is said, "If you don't go within, you will go without." As you move toward being an active, conscious co-creator in your own life, the most important thing you can do relative to this law is to examine the way you think. Change the quality of your thoughts, and you will change the quality of your life.

4. **The Law of Belief:** The law of belief states that whatever is in your belief system, whether with feeling and conviction or not, becomes your reality. It is not until you change your belief system that you can begin to change your reality and your performance. This is fact. It is not negotiable—that is the way it works. You were designed this way for very good reason, so you can learn through experience. The quicker you learn, the easier it becomes for you. Your thoughts (energy) are determined largely by the quality of your beliefs, which in turn form your perceptions, which are then broadcast outward into the infinite field of wave energy, much like a radio frequency.

Then transformed waves (spiritual realm) turn into particles (matter) and join together with additional energies that vibrate at a harmonious frequency and collectively join to shape what you come to see and experience in the physical world. You quite literally have the ability to mold and shape the various areas of your life based on how you choose to think, believe, and feel. In a nutshell, whatever you think about and believe to be true, regardless if those beliefs are based on "real" truth or perceived truth, are what determines how your life will unfold. The law of belief, when understood and practiced, can help anyone to manifest those things in life that one truly wants. There is a prerequisite, however: you must first find and release the old belief systems within you before you program yourself with the new. We will be covering some how to's on this in the next section on road blocks. In programming, new beliefs, you do need absolute clarity on your objectives, a basic plan to get you there, and then you must believe that you are destined to achieve them. Lastly, you must continuously reinforce these beliefs in your own mind. When your beliefs are firmly cemented in and harmonize with your goals, you have deep-seated faith. That which you "see" in the unseen is already yours.

5. **The Law of Vibration:** This law states that anything and everything that exists in our universe (seen or unseen), when broken down into and analyzed in its purest and most basic form, consists of pure energy that resonates and exists as a vibratory frequency or pattern. All matter, thoughts, and feelings have their own vibrational frequencies. The thoughts, feelings, and actions we choose also have their own particular rates of vibration. These vibrations will set up resonance with whatever possesses identical frequency. In other words, your thoughts are inseparably connected to the rest of the universe.

Like attracts like. As you choose good thoughts, more good thoughts of a like nature will follow, and you will also be in vibrational harmony with others with like thoughts. Modern science tells us that everything in the manifest universe is ultimately composed of packets of energy, quantized units vibrating at specific frequencies. In essence, everything is comprised of energy and empty space. Everything that appears solid is the frequency of the vibration of the energy that makes it up. For us, thought is where it all begins. As your conscious mind dwells, habitually on thoughts of a certain quality, these become firmly imbedded in the subconscious mind; they become the dominant vibration. This dominant vibration sets up a resonance with other similar vibrations and draws them into your life. Consider from a metaphysical view this very important point. The whole universe is mind. In turn, your vibrations affect everything around you—your environment, the people, animals, and even plants around you—and in turn, they affect you. Your feeling at the present moment dictates your vibration. It is said that feeling is a word to define conscious vibration. Therefore, your feeling at the moment is your vibration you are in, which sets up things of like nature. Positive feelings equal positive circumstances, and negative feelings equal negative circumstances. It is paramount that you be in the right vibrational frequency (frame of mind) as you are visualizing or meditating on that which you are choosing to co-create or manifest in your life.

6. **The Law of Action (Inspired):** The law of action must be employed in order for us to manifest things on earth. We must engage in actions that support our thoughts, dreams, emotions, and words. The law of action states that you must do the things and perform the actions necessary to achieve what you are setting out to do. Unless you take actions that are in

harmony with your thoughts and dreams and proceed in an orderly fashion towards what you want to accomplish, there will be absolutely no foreseeable results. It is here, with the law of action, that most people falter when pursuing success. There are two main reasons for this failure. First, the actions themselves must be inspired actions and should not be random actions. When preparing to take a particular action toward your goal, check in with your emotional guidance system, your heart, to confirm that it feels right. Your ego, or conscious thinking mind, most often produce random actions. When you operate from your heart, you are harmonizing with your higher self that is true spirit and one with God. On the other hand, your ego, otherwise known as Edging God Out, may very well produce wasted actions that will bring failure. Of course, the second reason for failure is fear, or plain laziness to take action. In this case, when you are in the beginning stages of making a serious change or are attempting to manifest something into your life, the desire for that change had best be hot. When you take action from the smallest thing, such as writing a to-do list in the morning, you set into motion corresponding effects that change your immediate future. If you follow up day after day, it can become a way of living, and the results will be exponential. It's obvious by now that building the framework for that which you wish to bring from the unseen into your physical experience consists of steps that are largely mental, observing and following these universal laws and principles. This particular law of action will require you to push that framework into the water to test its strength and readiness. Use shallow waters at first, making necessary adjustments, and then with a little more inspired action, away you go.

7. **The Law of Detachment:** The law of detachment says that in order to successfully attract something to you, you must be detached to the outcome. This is probably the most difficult law to come to grips with and implement in your co-creation process, because it seems all too inconsistent with the law of attraction. On the contrary, the law of detachment is complimentary to the law of attraction. If you are attached, you project negative emotions of fear, doubt, or craving, which attract the opposite of your desire. You are operating from a position of worry, fear, and doubt rather than serenity, trust, and faith. Let go and let God. Anything you want can be acquired through detachment, because detachment is based on resting in the complete grace of God and knowing that He is always working everything through you and together for your greatest good. To be detached is to realize that everything good is from the God Force, and nothing at all is from you. It is the Creator creating through you and the other elements in your reality, so there's nothing to hold on to as your own; all you have to do is to have the right beliefs and let God do it. You have to take your conscious mind off of it so that your subconscious mind can take over. All creation is subjective. To detach is to allow the universe to bring your desire into manifestation whichever way is best for you. When you are detached, your desires will manifest much faster. Realize that there is an infinite intelligence working alongside your own, and it is the one that can bring you a better way or more worthwhile experience. All you have to do is state your intensions and desires, and detach from the how and when they manifest. The law of detachment accelerates the whole process of evolution. When you understand this law, you don't feel compelled to force situations.

8. **The Law of Gratitude:** The law of gratitude plays out similar to the law of cause and effect, or the natural principle of action and reaction. As we look at the law itself, when we express thankfulness to the God Force for that which we have "received" (even though it is still in the unseen), it is an expenditure of force, and therefore our gratitude cannot fail to reach God; when it does, the reaction is an instantaneous move toward you. Consider two properly aligned magnets. They are two forces moving in opposite directions while moving toward one another. Gratitude draws you and the creative force, God, directly toward each other. If our gratitude is strong enough and consistent, then there will always be a move of that which we are co-creating toward us. When the God Force moves toward us, it brings all that it is. The law of gratitude also dictates that if our hearts are not full of gratitude, then something else will take its place. Physics teaches that nature will not tolerate a vacuum. That is to say, if something is removed, then something else must take its place. If our hearts are not filled with gratitude, then our hearts will be filled with ungratefulness. An ungrateful heart will take you from what you want as rapidly as a grateful heart will take you toward what you want. The law of gratitude nourishes our faith because as a grateful heart and mind continually expects good things, expectation becomes faith. This faith then becomes both the cornerstone and the capstone of what it is we are building, which comes only from our universal supplier, God. Gratitude toward God has the power to produce supernatural results, remove obstacles in the path of your destiny, and release creative power to produce what you want. There is no doubt that an attitude of gratitude is a must in your quest to co-create.

So, there you have it: the eight universal laws that I feel you should at least be aware of and that take a role in the process of co-creation, or what we like to call manifesting. I do realize that they do have a similarity to one another, and in some respects, one produces the other and so on, but it is after all about harmony and balance, don't you think?

I know what you're probably thinking. "This stuff is all well and good, but I grabbed your book because I wanted to learn how to manifest stuff in my life. I wanted to learn how to make some major changes. I wanted to learn how to improve myself and maybe get unstuck from my humdrum life, and so far, I'm reading about God, the beginning of creation, and universal laws! That's all great but, can we get to it?"

I have a question for you. Have you ever watched a good painter paint a beautiful landscape scene? They always start with the background and work inward, to the more detailed figures. The background sets the tone for the completed picture. What you're looking to do here relative to making changes in your life is awesome, and I commend you for that decision, however it is no small task. From what we've covered so far, we are putting in the background if you will. Co-creating is something we unconsciously do to some degree or another. But when we consciously try to make changes, all of a sudden, it's difficult. It's difficult because we don't know the rules. We probably never stopped to think about the fact that it's a process. You need to see the internal workings of the manifesting machine. Again, that's why you've read what you've read thus far. Bear with me; it will all make sense and come together like the pieces of a puzzle.

If you were to take a random survey to people on the street and ask if they were completely happy with themselves and their lives, how many of them do you suppose would tell you that they were? Oh, I'm sure a few are, but the vast majority would certainly like a thing or two to change in their personal lives, their professional lives, or their financial picture. Now, ask them why don't they go ahead and make those changes. What answers do you get? My guess is some would attest that they've tried, but nothing has worked for them. Some may say that they don't quite know how to go about it. A few would probably tell you that they fear going out beyond their current safety zone to explore that unknown territory. A few more may say that it's a nice thought, but they don't feel that they deserve those lofty dreams. This is not to say that if you have a decent job, a home, and a loving family and are relatively comfortable in your lifestyle that there is anything wrong with that. On the contrary, you are already a success on many levels for sure. Success in and of itself has a different face for different people. Only you can define your own version. However, if you have that little something inside you that is pulling and nagging at you to be seen, felt, and heard from, and you are not experiencing it, then it is up to you to decide to do what you can to breathe life into it. Chances are pretty good that that's where you are; otherwise, you probably wouldn't have been attracted to this book. Refer to the laws of attraction and correspondence.

You've come to a decision that something's got to change, and you are going to make the effort to produce some form of change and you want to manifest this as soon as possible. Get real with yourself about this journey. Know without a doubt that you will need to take a hard look at this next section and deal with it before you attempt to co-create the desires of your heart.

SECTION 3

Roadblocks

I'm assuming you've identified what it is that you would either like to change or manifest in a particular area of your life. Some of you have always kind of known; others have just come to realize you can expand outward and have and or be more for yourself and your family. As you take the time to visualize yourself having, doing, or being that which you desire, get in touch with the emotions attached to that vision. What have you got? Excitement, I hope. That would be the best feeling as you look at yourself with this new desire as your own. Dig deeper—what else? Chances are you feel a little fear, maybe? Are you not sure just how this is going to happen? After all, you may have always thought it would be nice, but now that you're going for it for real, this unknown territory is scary stuff. Maybe a little doubt is creeping in there? "I'm not sure if I can do this. I'm not good enough." Maybe some old, haunting words from your past come up. "You'll never amount to anything! You're a dreamer, not a doer. You've failed before—why should this work?" The list can be endless. Meet some of your roadblocks on the road to co-creating.

Truth be told, it's easy to get excited about making some changes in your life. Heck, I remember being dazzled by various motivational speakers when I was looking for change. They struck a chord within me and lit a fire to the fact that I could be what I wanted to be, do what I wanted to do, and have what I wanted to have. The trouble was when I put the rubber to the road with my idea, and obstacles came up that I didn't know how to handle, the air was taken out of my sails, and I coasted to a halt. I labeled myself a failure, and that hurt. Then others labeled me a failure, and that hurt worse. Where was my motivation now? Chalk up another hash mark on the negative side of venturing out beyond my comfort zone. How dare I think beyond what God had given me! Who was I to think I could have more? If God wanted me to be rich, I'd have been born into a rich family, right? I had it pretty good now, so I should just let this pipe dream go and be "normal."

Manifesting or co-creating during our lifetimes is our God-given ability. It's perfectly proper in our walk of physical life. We seem to do it easy enough for the simple wants of life without even thinking we're doing it. Now, all of a sudden, we think a little further out of the box for something beyond the norm, and it not only seems difficult but dredges up all the reasons why not, which usually come from our past history or programming from earlier years.

If you are going to make the decision to move forward, test your true power, and claim your true self, then you'd better have a clear road on which to travel to this exciting and rewarding life experience. You must have an unobstructed view of that which you want to bring to you. If a road construction crew is to build a road through a wooded area, they don't just lay down the asphalt without first removing the brush, trees, rocks, and any other obstructions. The way must be clear, the ground must be firm, and the materials should be tested and proven. Obviously, no less care should be taken on your part as you begin your journey to expand in whatever direction you feel important for you.

It's an exhilarating feeling once you decide to make a change in your life and bring your heart's desire from thought into your physical experience. Right here, at the starting gate, is where you have to check your bags, if you will, and determine what might be your possible roadblocks to the finish line. You need to be as light and unencumbered as possible. Any negative feelings or emotions about what you are doing will become very heavy and will slow you down, if they don't stop you all together.

We should start with your self-talk. This is the obvious place to check because you are with yourself twenty-four seven, and that marvelous transmitter that is inside your skull and between your ears is continuously thinking and receiving cosmic vibrations from everywhere. Most of the message of this very book is about awareness. What I'm suggesting is that you start right now and become aware of how you talk to yourself. Is the general flow of your thinking positive, upbeat, hopeful, and loving toward yourself or others? Or is it negative, morose, doubtful, fearful, or hateful? You must make a conscious effort to notice this self-talk so you can learn to stop it in its tracks and change the direction of that thought flow. Remember that thoughts, even what you may consider minor or unintentional ones, are creative; with enough time and repetition, they can become imbedded into your subconscious, and then it becomes your belief system. Remember the law of belief? Remember that if your self-talk is negative at this point, it certainly will be inconsistent with what you are trying to bring to you. Ultimately, you will be taking one step forward and two steps back.

Negative self-talk, or stinking thinking as it's known, usually has its roots in your self-esteem. Self-esteem is nothing more than the sum total of who you are on an emotional level based on all you've encountered. If that includes difficult times, then the lofty thought of making a serious change in your life or bringing something you really want to you may look like a mountain you can't climb. Simply sit quietly and focus on the possibility of a loving relationship you'd enjoy being in, or on improving the one you're currently in, or on a career move that seems exciting, not to mention the thoughts of becoming financially free. These are great, but if you have low self-esteem, what happens here? You may let yourself step forward to begin the process because initially you're excited about the possibilities, but before you know it, those old, negative programs will surface, and because the process you are embarking on isn't instantaneous and takes time, it leaves plenty of time for the old dream killer, doubt, to show itself. Unless you are absolutely confident that what you are looking at in your visual imagery is already yours, then you have doubt. Think of doubt, fear, and skepticism as the neutral gear in your car. You're driving down the road, and you put your vehicle in neutral. Immediately the forward momentum is no longer, and you will eventually coast to a stop. Let me go on to say that what I've described is pretty normal for most folks in some fashion, but it still needs to be addressed before you can successfully co-create or manifest change.

A number of years ago, a book and a corresponding movie came out called *The Secret*. It caused quite a stir and was responsible for a considerable movement in the law of attraction and the manifestation arena. As a metaphysician and complimentary health care practitioner, I too jumped on that train. I knew that this secret wasn't really a secret at all; it's simply that the majority of the population wasn't aware of the law of attraction. Nonetheless I still needed to see what it was all about. All in all, I felt that it was put together reasonably well despite a few holes. It brought a degree of excitement to readers and viewers relative to the possibilities at hand, if they simply followed these steps in this "hidden secret."

After a period of time of working with what the book or movie was suggesting, the general consensus was that none of it really worked to any great degree. The public at large wasn't seeing what they wanted to manifest. Many were left dismayed and defeated because this "magic" law of attraction failed to bring their much-anticipated results.

As an adjunct to this review, I will tell you that I remember sharing my copies of both the book and the movie to several of my clients at that time as a must-see if they were serious about making life changes. What was different with my people was that we had filled in the holes that were in the process described in the material, which was dealing with their negative self-talk, doubt, fear, and skepticism first before they ventured into the process. My clients had a leg up from the beginning because this delicate but important area had been addressed. Various behavioral modifications, stress, anxiety, anger, and fear, to name a few issues, were dealt with in order to give these individuals a clearer focus and a more positive outlook on getting what they wanted relative to changes. We built up their self-esteem enough to allow themselves to accept both their new image, and to feel good enough to bring something of value into their lives. Understand that you must be able to see yourself being, having, or doing the thing you are looking to co-create, and from that image you are able to emotionalize, which is the vital active ingredient.

I've told you all that to tell you this: identify your roadblocks! You have things in your past that may have the potential to sabotage the good you want from coming to you. Be honest with yourself. Be your harshest critic. This is preparing the foundation of your future. You can't build a house on quicksand, and neither can you plant a garden that is filled with weeds.

Consider that you are now the sum total of everything you've ever done, seen, and experienced. Run a playback of your life in your mind's eye like an old movie, and wherever there was a situation, circumstance, or event that may have been the least bit tragic or upsetting, stop and write it down. Continue to write down anything negative that pops up. After collecting all that you've written down, go back and look—I mean *really* look at each one. Determine honestly if it has any real effect on who you are right now. How much (if any) power does it have over you? Does that event cause you to doubt yourself? Is there any guilt there? Does forgiveness need to come into the picture? Are you still hiding from something?

Do you see where I'm going with this? Anything that came into your life experience that was negative in some fashion, and that hasn't been neutralized, has the power to cause you to feel unworthy or not good enough to actually have or become this desire of your heart. Going from the origin to the present, it looks like this: The traumatic event can be anything that impacts you in a negative way, such as being embarrassed, put down, abandoned, abused, or frightened. This hits your life at a particular time and stops you in your tracks, from just a few moments to years. Whatever it was leaves you with a memory that is naturally negative and uncomfortable when you think back to it. This is an emotion with a negative and powerful effect on you that you own because it is has scared you on a cellular level. In some cases, it has become subjective because you've grown up around it and don't think consciously about it on a regular basis, but because it's subjective, you may now have stinking thinking. A part of you on a conscious level wants to manifest something really exciting and life-changing now, but subjectively you don't because doing so would mean you were becoming something you don't really believe you should be. There is one other emotional pothole that can have a growth-stunting effect on some, and that is not meeting someone else's expectations for your life. Usually some loving and well-meaning figures such as a parents, spouses, or teachers may have had some vision for you that they felt would be good for you, or they'd like to see you doing, but your heart isn't in it. If you dare to think outside of that, it could bring on guilt. Although not really traumatic, it is a powerful negative force that's inconsistent with your heart's desire at this time.

Now, I'm not saying that every little negative experience you've encountered in your lifetime has to be the enemy here. In some cases, you may have learned a very valuable lesson and become a much better and stronger person as a result of it. For the most part, those won't even show themselves as you think back on your life in introspection; they are like small pebbles on the road. What you're looking for are the boulders, and you'll know them because they will stick out and show themselves. I know you may have been hiding from them for years, trying your best to not go there and to bury them deeper as the year's march on. I get it. It's part of your survival mechanism, and if you are happy with the status quo in your life now, I'd say, "Fine, carry on." However, the simple fact is that you are here, reading this book, is because you do want significant change to take place in your life. You want to co-create or manifest something exciting, am I right? Then this stuff has to be brought to the light of day, dealt with, and neutralized so that it no longer has a subjective effect on who or what you are, and so you can march forward to any destination you choose without looking over your shoulder.

Now, how do you deal with such things? I assume you've done the hard part and maybe let the lion out of the cage. I will throw out my perspective on dealing with your emotional roadblocks to your co-creating. Understand that there are many roads to the mansion here, and I'm not suggesting that my view is the only solution. Hear me out, think it through, and listen to your heart. Remember, the heart is where your truth lives. The brain is there to help you process. They must work in harmony.

By now you know my background as a metaphysician and complimentary health practitioner. My original tool of choice for dealing with such difficulties or negative behaviors, memories, and wounds was hypnosis. Scary as that may sound to some, it's always been a viable modality to initiate change simply because it's designed to work on the subjective level where the origins of such problems still live on. Getting to the initial sensitizing event is paramount. From there, you come to realize that it's not who you are any longer. You can bring in forgiveness for both any possible antagonist and yourself, and then you can understand the lesson and move on peacefully. This is known as regression therapy, and the hypnotist is gently guiding you back to the origin and helping you to unwrap the story, as well as bring it to a wholesome ending.

Just so you understand, hypnosis is a very natural state of mind. Providing we are of a healthy mental capacity, we all experience a form of hypnosis every day—several times a day, I might add. In falling off to sleep or waking up, we pass through what's known as the hypnogogic state. We're not quite fully awake, but we're not yet asleep either. The state may be fleeting, but it is real. The same experience happens when we are engrossed in a movie, and we suspend our belief systems for the benefit of moving along with the storyline of the movie. Possibly it happens while at work, and we stop to gaze off into the distance for a few moments of mental escape, not thinking of anything in particular. Starring into a fire is another doorway into a hypnotic state. So, you see, there is nothing to fear should you choose to utilize hypnosis with a trained and experienced hypnotist. Hypnotists become guides to gently and naturally bring you to a relaxed state where your brain vibrations decrease from beta level to alpha level; then the critical factor of the conscious mind goes into the background, and your subjective mind is accessible. Here lives the file cabinet of everything you've ever experienced through any of your five senses. Every emotion (good, bad, or otherwise) has a story. Our conscious thinking minds don't need to clutter up with every tidbit of this data, so they get filed away to the subconscious after time. Every silly little experience is retrievable.

One more important note here relative to hypnosis: when re-experiencing something that was traumatic in your past during a regression session, nothing from that experience can ever harm you. You are never vulnerable to any input from a hypnotist that is contrary to your morals, values, or core beliefs. You are in total control, can let go of whatever you are ready to let go of, and accept only what you feel you want to accept. In saying that, I would add something I used to tell my perspective clients. Hypnosis doesn't work—you do. Hypnosis is nothing more than a state of mind where your mental garden can be weeded and replanted with whatever you choose.

Moving along, I have one more tool that I began to use on negative emotions. This tool came along several years after I was successfully using hypnosis. In fact, when it came around, I redesigned my practice to utilize it in some cases with hypnosis, and eventually it became a stand-alone therapeutic process that I insisted every client learn and take home. It was designed to be a self-healing modality.

We're now talking about emotional freedom technique, or EFT for short. Considered a universal healing aid, EFT is based on impressive new discoveries involving the body's subtle energies and the theory that the cause of all negative emotions is a disruption in the body's energy system.

Remember when we talked about the fact that we are really spiritual beings in a human physical experience, and that thoughts are vibrational frequencies? Well, we are in fact energy beings, and this healing modality works directly with this part of our makeup. There are fourteen major meridians that run through our body. These are not physical but electrical tracks that carry our thought vibrations throughout the body. That explains why your body responds or reacts the way it does to positive or negative thoughts. Obviously, positive thoughts bring a good or happy feeling to the body, whereas negative thoughts bring dark, heavy, or ill feelings to the body. When the brain transmits a negative thought, it creates a kind of kink or blockage in one or more of the meridians. At this point, you are in disharmony emotionally, and if left unattended, it will affect your body because everything is connected. The Chinese have known this for hundreds of years and developed acupuncture, which places pressure on these meridians using needles, to unblock the energy flow and restore the body to health.

EFT mirrors acupuncture in that it unblocks various energy meridians that hold uncomfortable or traumatic thought emotions. The difference is that needles are not used. Neither are drugs or any equipment required. Instead, it consists of a series of gentle finger tapings on the endpoints of the major meridians, together with a learned algorithm. Using EFT with my clients, I saw a 98-100% effective rate. Many significant studies are available at EFT sites on line that will confirm my findings. The whole process is easily learned and can be quickly applied anytime there is a need for immediate relief from something that is troubling. It can also be used to go back in introspection to your past and address old issues that still affect you emotionally when you think about them. With this knowledge and know-how, you can become your own therapist.

So, there you have it: two possible ways you can deal with issues that, based on your honest assessment of yourself, could stand in your way to co-creating a better picture for yourself. If you choose to utilize either of the modalities I've explained here in this section, please be mindful and seek a professional who is well versed in either hypnosis and regression therapy, as well as EFT. With hypnosis, you would need the one-on-one to get the resolve you seek, but with EFT, once you've learned the process from someone who understands it, you can pretty much fly on your own with it.

Just to summarize, I've chosen to devote this section of my book to roadblocks, along with a couple of tools I've had experience with to remove them for a very important reason. I'd be remiss if I didn't. All of us have been blessed with the ability to co-create—no exceptions. We simply need to become aware of that ability. Think of it as a treasure chest buried deep within us. However, on top of that chest lies the debris of ignorance and the weeds of negative beliefs, thoughts, and conditioning. This is not to mention any personal life experiences that may have damaged our self-worth and prevent it from even thinking of claiming a better scenario for ourselves.

The bottom line is when you deal with all your negatives and make them disappear for good, then you'll notice that your manifestations happen even before you ask for them. This state of awareness couldn't possibly happen until you are fully clean and clear, devoid of roadblocks and brick walls. Herein lies the most important part relative to your ability to co-create!

SECTION 4

Steps

As we move on now, let's take a look at what we've covered so far regarding this co-creation topic, and show it in a digestible step by step process. Please note, however, that the reality is more an awareness of a process in order to bring successful change into your life. With the awareness, all you need do is allow universal law to do what it does.

1. Recognize Who You Really Are

Find a nice mirror. Sit comfortably in front of it and look at that reflection of you. Stare at it. No, seriously—really look deeply at every bit of you that comes into view. Look at the magnificence of that human creation. Consider your breathing, your heartbeat, and the blinking of your eyes. Are you consciously doing those things? How about your current thoughts? Where are they coming from? Can you bring yourself to see that you are more than what is bouncing back from that mirror? Look beyond the physical to the essence of you, your very consciousness. You are a creation of the Creator, and therefore you're a part of the Creator. You are an expression of universal consciousness. The consciousness of you is temporarily manifesting itself in individual form through your body. There is only one consciousness here; it is you and me and all things both visible and invisible. Everywhere you go, you are staring into a different reflection of yourself. Remember that you, in your physical body, are an extension of that which we call God. Because you are the furthermost extension of the Source, God is also experiencing that expansion because of you, through you, and with you. Please own that, because it is truth. Begin to touch in with your vast power and the possibilities that you can do with it.

2. Determine That Which You Are Choosing to Manifest

There is never a time in people's lives, regardless of who they are or what circumstances they come from, that the feeling of want or need doesn't arise. Obviously, for small, everyday type things, in most cases they can be fulfilled relatively easily. We don't have to do too much outside of recognizing the need, and making the physical effort to go get it or do it. It may take a few days, but if it's enough of a priority, it will usually be ours in good time. That is manifesting for sure, but what we are talking about here lies in larger areas of change such as job changes or a loving relationship, be it a new one or an improvement of a current one. Is it something relative to your health, perhaps? And there's always a need for a sudden infusion of cash for reasons you deem important: various fun things, a new car, a vacation, or maybe even the home of your dreams. You get the idea—anything that you can have, do, or be that may be a bit too big for our everyday process to go get. Running out to the store for a new car isn't as easy as going to Wal-Mart for that new pair of jeans you need. Whatever will bring some form of improvement to you and or your family would go here. I have a feeling you already know what you'd like to co-create, so let's continue.

3. Visualize Yourself Having, Doing, or Being That Which You've Chosen

This is the first time you do this, but it's certainly not the last. At this point, you are looking to see just how comfortable you feel with this new reality. Realistically, if you went out to buy a new suit or dress, I'm sure you'd want to try it on first before you made the investment. This is big stuff here; have fun with "owning" it in your mind's eye. It's what you want, isn't it?

4. Identify Blockages

At this point, you more than likely will start to find or hear reasons why not. The more you put yourself into the picture of this completed manifestation in your visualization, the more the thoughts coming off the analytical side of your thinking will begin to toss the pros and cons. This is important, and you should look closely at both, possibly even taking the time to write them down. As long as your pros outweigh the cons, and you've determined that this is coming more from your heart rather than your ego, then look and listen a little deeper. Listen for any of that negative self-talk we looked at earlier. Do you deserve it? Are you good enough and smart enough? Do you really believe you can? Just how is this going to happen? What will others think? This list is open-ended, and you may have multiple negative feelings, emotions, and fears relative to what you are choosing to manifest. Please don't short-change this area because it is the foundation on which you build.

5. Derail and Neutralize Manifestation Blocks

Obviously, not every negative feeling you encounter from the previous step will be of major proportions. Some you may be able to neutralize quite naturally on your own, by simply being aware of it and making conscious effort to think differently regarding it.

Others may be deeper wounds that mere conscious effort won't touch. Here you need to determine what process you need to employ, be it on your own or with professional help. I mentioned a couple that I'm personally familiar with, but again, whatever you feel is more comfortable for you would be in your best interest. Keep in mind the goal here. Think of it this way: your idea or desire is similar to an unborn child, tucked safely in the womb of your mind. You will do everything in your power to protect it and make sure it is loved and nourished with good food until it's ready to show itself in your world and stand on its own. I don't mean to make this sound difficult, but you must be clear and free to manifest properly. Be vigilant in the pursuit of negativity.

6. Verbalize Your Statement of Intent

Here, you simply put your goal into a statement of intent and verbalize it. An example would be, "I am now the manager of my department, and it is so!" Or, "I am now enjoying my new car, and it is so!" It can be short, to the point, and in the now as you are already experiencing it. The reason for this—and you don't have to spend a lot of time here—is so you can capture the immediate feeling you get from saying it. Check to make sure you are completely comfortable with it emotionally. If for any reason, you're not, I suggest you go back and fix it before we move on.

7. Building Your Etheric Model

Now the rubber meets the road. It's time to put everything together, and in order to do that, we need a workshop, if you will. I like to call it the workshop of the mind, or a mental sanctuary. Make no mistake, this is a very special and sacred ground, so I want to convey that it would be a good idea to introduce you to the idea of meditation. Easy does it; it's not all that complicated, and you're only going to spend a few minutes at a time once or maybe twice a day in this quiet space. The reason is simple. Remember when we spoke of the fact that all physical manifestations came from nowhere to now here? Everything was first a thought before it was a thing. Those thoughts are a part of the source consciousness, of God. You are now on the doorstep of the creation of a thing you want in your life. In order to do that, you need to connect to the Source on as many levels of self as you can, allowing the Source to work through you to bring you what you desire. The best way to do that is to go to the place where the Source lives. That, my friend, is in silence. Silence speaks louder than words. In silence, you become fertile ground for inspiration. Prayer is talking to God, but inspiration is God talking to you. So again, we're not going to make a big process out of this—no incense, no humming, no chanting, no candles or bells. You don't have to sit cross-legged on the floor. Simply enter the quiet and be still.

First, you need a time that works best for you. Preferably, when you won't be disturbed by others, or outside distractions. I find early mornings work best for me, but you may prefer evenings before bed. As you get more use to this, you'll be able to more easily tune out outside distractions if you can't totally find the right space. For now, while you are introducing this to yourself, just get as much total quiet as you can. Next, I recommend you find a comfortable place to sit upright, with your feet flat on the floor and your back supported. Close your eyes, take a deep breath, hold it for three to five seconds, and let it slowly out for as many seconds. Do this no less than three times and let go more and more each time, settling into a natural, relaxed state. Stay focused on your breathing in and out, in and out. As you continue with your breathing, random thoughts will be ever present, but you need to let them go. What works for me is picturing my head with both of my temples open like windows on either side of a house. See a thought float in and notice it, and it floats back out the other window. It's next to impossible to stop thoughts, so this way you notice them come and go without holding on to any one in particular. With each out breath, you are deeper relaxed, and the quiet becomes you.

Now you can begin to focus on what you want to co-create. You see it as already yours; you and it are now one. You are doing, being, or enjoying this desire of yours. Bring it into view with as much clarity as you possibly can. As you focus on the finished picture, bring in the emotion you'd have because you know it is now yours. Remember, emotion (energy plus motion) is the accelerant that brings it to you quicker. Try to stay with this emotional image for just a couple minutes, repeat the words "It is so" three times, and let yourself naturally emerge from that state. You've just built a spiritual image of what you want to manifest, and you're proclaimed that it is in fact yours.

8. It is So, Let Go and Know

From beginning to end, you may have ten to fifteen minutes invested in building within the confines of your mental sanctuary. Do this daily with conviction. The three most important aspects of this are: Repeating "It is so!" after your imagery. Here is the law of inspired action; you have declared what you set out to do. It is done. Then let it go. There's no need to focus further on this for the day; go about your business. Here is the law of detachment. Finally, know, your heart has no doubt. It's an absolute done deal. This is the law of belief.

By now you're probably saying, "Wow, I've got to remember all this information and all these steps in order to be a co-creator!" My answer would be no. Being a co-creator to manifest various changes or to bring various physical things into your current life experience isn't necessarily about steps. As you explore this whole concept and read different materials about manifesting, there will be different approaches and guidelines. It's good to be familiar with as much as you choose. Ultimately, it's about awareness that there is a process, and once you recognize that and become a clear vessel, the process works naturally through you, easily and effortlessly. Jesus once said, "Know the truth, and the truth will set you free." There is only one thing to be set free from, and that is ignorance!

It's important to remember that it is never about making things happen; it's always about allowing things to happen. One can't grab water because it quickly runs out of your grasp, but you can in fact hold water by gently cupping it into your palm. By allowing, you are being okay in every way with whatever is going on. You are detached from worrying about how it's going to happen. Know this: 99.99 percent of your creation is complete before you see any physical evidence of it. This is so hard for us humans to accept because we've been programmed to the old saying "I'll believe it when I see it." I suggesting you adopt a new saying: "Because I believe it, I will see it!"

9. Don't Just Do Something—Sit There

As will be explained in more depth a bit later in the section on bonus laws, I've included this piece in the steps to help clarify the importance of both action and inaction, which oddly enough are vital ingredients in the co-creation process. Lao Tzu said, "All things are possible to him that can practice inaction." This doesn't mean that we are to sit and do nothing. On the contrary, it means that we are to let go into the natural flow of life. You're going to get excited about taking an active part in your co-creation project, as you should. Whenever you are prompted to do something to help it along, don't just do something—sit there. Take it into the still, small voice and listen for the answer. Trust that the answer will come, and confirm it is inspired action you are hearing. You will do the right thing at just the right time. Remember that you have the Creator within you; you don't have to go looking for It. All you have to do is to be still and know that It is right where you are.

Know that you are abundantly supported. Know that all you desire is the Creator's good pleasure to give you. You are magnificent and spectacular. You are the way God shows Its love for the world. Trust the divine wisdom within yourself to guide you to your greatest yet to be. Let go of your need to make it happen. Allow spirit to perfect the work appointed to you. Everything is well. Be at peace.

SECTION 5

Bonus Exercise

Sixty-Eight Seconds

I have to tell you that over the years in private practice, one of the most frustrating things I had to deal with was the fact that even though people had very legitimate issues, problems, and circumstances they wanted to deal with, and even though they did in fact take the initiative to come to me for possible resolve, they were still lazy. I don't mean that in a condescending way. It's human nature for us to look for the quick fix for just about everything. We don't necessarily want to do the work that it takes to get the job done. We look for the magic pill for the cure of our problems. Hey, I'm no different and have fallen into that pit myself. As I said, it's human nature to look for shortcuts. The truth is that in the arena of self-help or self-improvement, there is no magic pill. You have to dig into some difficult areas and get your hands dirty. You have to do some work if you want results.

Look at where you are right now, reading and learning about the process of co-creation, for heaven's sakes. That's certainly more involved and in depth than dealing with smoking cessation or losing twenty pounds.

You're learning about the process of bringing something into your life experience that is an idea or a desire. You have to become one with that. You have to be a clear vessel for that. It takes time and effort on your part. It takes honest introspection into the deepest parts of you. It's no small task, and we've covered a lot of ground so far to help you see the big picture and know what to do and how to do it.

I haven't found any magic pills in all this, but what I want to share with you now is what may appear to you as a shortcut to the results you seek. I found the following exercise a few years ago, in my work with the law of attraction. I can attest to the fact that it is very powerful and works wonders, but by no means does it give you special dispensation from taking the trash out relative to any negativity and blockages. You still must be that clear vessel for this to do the job it can do. You should feel happy when you do this exercise. You should feel a strong emotion inside of yourself as you feel already in possession of whatever it is you are choosing to bring in.

The sixty-eight-second technique for attracting your desire can be utilized like a laser treatment after you understand all the components and laws of the process of co-creation itself. That way you will be actually able to see the process at work. This is really an exercise that is an extension of step seven in the previous section. The author of the following exercise used the example of bringing a certain amount of money into your life, so for the sake of ease and simplicity, I'll follow suit and pass along that example. Obviously, you'll have to get a little creative and inject your specific desire into this picture. Remember, the basis of this is to deliberately flow energy and raise your vibration to connect with that which you desire.

Look at the second hand on a watch or a clock, and prepare to time yourself for seventeen seconds. You've determined that you want a certain amount of money to possess every month. Be specific here, be it money, job, health, a relationship, or a material item. Visualize counting out the money that you've determined you want to flow into your life. Feel the money in your hands right now, not in the future. Count it. It feels good, doesn't it? Rub it all over your physical body. You are bringing in your senses. What takes place will now change your life forever. By bringing in and practicing the next two techniques, you will know how you can change and create anything you want to experience in your life. Those first seventeen seconds are gone.

As you start the next seventeen seconds, smell the money, rubbing it in your nose. Keep smelling the money until you can feel the paper money actually tickle the end of your nose. Those seventeen seconds are gone. Now taste the money, and lick the money until feel the money on your tongue. Keep going back and forth on the fanned-out amount of money that you have in your hands with your tongue. Keep doing these three different techniques over and over until sixty-eight seconds or more have passed. You have just activated what worlds are made of. You have just activated the whole universe to help you bring into the physical world whatever amount of money that you want to come to you. You now have the keys to achieving anything you want to come to you in an effortless way.

According to the author of this technique, this is what is happening; each 17 second interval of exercise is equivalent to 2,000 action hours. Now, you will ask, just what is an action hour? That's a good question. That really wasn't explained. It is my opinion that its meaning can only be likened to time spent thinking about achieving a particular goal and maybe adding in occasional affirmations to strengthen your thoughts. Working this exercise employs several physical senses which tend to heighten the emotion. These in turn, heighten the vibration. You are raising your vibration to match the vibration you'd emotionally experience by possessing that money in your physical reality.

After holding this vibration for sixty-eight seconds or more, the universe really kicks in on your behalf and, well, things begin to happen. You are engaging the law of attraction at its highest level. If you miss a day or two, no worries. It will not hurt anything; you'll simply slow down the desire from coming to you sooner. After you have practiced this exercise for a few weeks, know that you are now being guided on any subsequent actions. Because you have created 99 percent of the money in your visualization, the other 1 percent of the work will be through physical participation on your part. Detach yourself from the how of it; listen to the inspiration and allow.

Your current belief system may not allow you to fully believe that something like this exercise could possibly work. After all, how silly do you feel even visualizing smelling and licking money? I get it, and you're certainly not the only one who'd have that impression. I have personally tried this and have had a positive result on a small scale because that was my target for test purposes. Let's not forget that despite the fact that this appears as a shortcut to your desires, you still have to be that clear vessel. You've got everything negative to lose and everything positive to gain. Get going, and prove it to yourself!

SECTION 6

Bonus Laws

The Law of Perpetual Transmutation

This law explains that everything in the universe that we can see, hear, smell, taste, or touch, together with our emotions, is the manifestation of energy in various levels of vibration. The universe as a whole, and in its parts, has its existence in an ocean of motion. Motion is the only thing that is constant. Change is energy's only attribute, and because of it, there comes all that is apparent to our material senses. Energy is in a constant state of transmission and transmutation. It is the cause and effect of itself and can be neither created nor destroyed.

This law explains that the nonphysical level of life is always moving into physical form. The physical level of life is the manifestation of the nonphysical. Emotions are expressed with and through the body. The body is moved into action, which produces the results.

This law explains the creative process. It also explains prayer. Prayer is the movement that takes place between spirit and form with and through you. This prayer I refer to is not one of supplication, (please give me...), but rather prayer of gratitude, (thank you for...).

The Law of God Action

There is a law in conscious creation of reality that is even higher than the law of attraction. It is the law of God action. It is the "secret" above *The Secret*. When you operate with the law of God action, you are operating at the highest level of all things, which is the level of spirit. It is the highest level that governs all other levels. When you work with the law of God action, you're not trying to create anything; you are simply allowing the universe to create through you. You are co-creating with God.

The law of God action states that God is the one who is acting through you. Therefore, there is nothing for you to do but allow God to do everything through you. It doesn't mean you do not take any action, but it means you do not take any action that you are not naturally guided from within to do. When you try to do things that you're not inspired to do, you are forcing action. The way of God action is to do non-doing action. It is to allow yourself to do what is seeking expression through you.

The problem with using the law of attraction alone, is that you are trying to manifest things and attempting to force energy to drive the creation process. The truth is that when you think you have to attract things, you are really saying that those things are outside of you. Actually, everything you desire is not outside of you—it is already in there and is waiting for you to open yourself to it. When you walk the path that the universe is guiding you to take, all the things you truly desire show up in divine time.

When you follow the law of God action, you will naturally use the law of attraction to draw into your space everything you need in every moment, without even trying to do so. That's because the universe has a plan for you, and by aligning yourself with that plan, you will synchronize your actions with the divine flow of events. You will find yourself doing the right thing at the right time and in the right place, where the resources or opportunities you require are already arranged to be there. You simply step right in.

You will hear that some people encounter failure in using the law of attraction. If you really look at it, their failure is really a conflict of intentions. You can manifest whatever you intend as long as it is according to the highest and best interest to all. Remember that you are not your individual consciousness alone; the real self is a collective whole that includes the entire universe, as well as the consciousness of your higher self.

The real self is pure spirit that is one with the spirit of God, or all that is. Upon your physical birth, you split a portion of your consciousness to be incarnated into this world with a purpose that you have planned. The conscious you that is here on earth is your lower self. All that you are meant to do and be is directed by your higher self through your true heart's desire. Act through your heart, not your head. When there is a conflict of intentions between your two selves, then you see failure of the law of attraction, and things don't manifest.

The most important thing you need to remember is to be in alignment with your higher self; that is when you are in harmony with the universe. Here is where you experience easy and effortless manifestation of all your true desires. The other reason for failed manifestation efforts is that not only are they not true desires of your heart, but you're not meant to intend them to happen at that moment. When you are intending the right thing at the right time, then you will experience spontaneous fulfillment.

Listen closely and read the following slowly. When you set an intention to create something, because of the law of duality, you are also creating the reality of its nonexistence. If it were there already, why would you have to create it? To resolve this duality of intention, you have to intend from a space of non-intention. "Wow, what the heck?" I hear you.

Slow down; it's okay. Listen, and place yourself in a state of consciousness where you already have everything you desire and there is nothing for you to do and nothing for you to create. Then from this place of non-desire, whatever desires that arise are desires from spirit. At this point, you are not trying to intend anything; you are simply allowing the intentions of the universe to flow to you. This is also known as creating from emptiness.

Living your life on purpose is the most important thing of all, and every goal or intention should be allowed to naturally arise from that place. The big question is, why do we spend so much time learning manifesting techniques? I would have to say that it makes you conscious of how you're creating reality, so you can co-create with the universe better, and allow the universe to create through you. Remember the ease with which the God Source created the world through the word, and it was so.

Remember the law of belief? If you believe it takes hard work to accomplish things, then that is what you will experience. If you believe things can be easy, effortless, and natural, then that is what you will experience. You really don't need to motivate yourself to do anything. All you need to do is to plug into the Source, and the energy will flow through you to do what you are here to do. You do not have to drive the system that runs you; you simply allow yourself to be driven by doing what you love now. You're here to do what brings you joy!

The law of God action is to go with the flow in every moment. When you follow your heart in every moment, you are connecting to the essence of who you really are, which is the power and the presence of God. The best action to do is non-doing action, which is doing things the natural way. This way, the law of God action is creating from the highest level.

The Law of Reversibility

This law explains why "faith is the substance of things hoped for, the evidence of things not seen." By bringing your state of mind to where it would be as you already have that which your desire, thus raising your vibration to the highest possible level of excitement. In other words, if a physical fact can produce a psychological state, then a psychological state can produce a physical fact.

The Law of Inverse Transformations

This law requires only that you evoke and sustain the feeling of your realized desire until your desire is realized. Witnessing an end result produces an equivalent emotion. Connecting with your desired goal on an emotional level first. Emotion mirrors action.

SECTION 7

Awareness and Quantum Physics

All of the material you've read here is not so much about the laws of creation or manifesting your desires. It's really more about awareness. You've now become aware of the idea that there is a process of co-creation, and that the laws are part of that co-creation process. You are also aware that in order for you to manifest change in a deliberate fashion, you must activate this process in a certain way of thought, behavior, and action.

My whole idea here was to bring you this awareness and break it down to its lowest common denomination, if you will, or its origin. I suppose it's like opening up the hood of your car and learning about how the engine works. With that information, you would have a more respectful knowledge of the real power that you command when you are behind the wheel.

Now, what about awareness itself? What happens when we become aware of anything? That brings us to a term you may have heard before. It's one that is gaining more presents in many aspects in today's language: quantum physics.

Quantum physics explains that everything is energy, waves of possibility, until it is observed. Once observed, the waves collapse into particles, and form is created. When we pay attention to anything (positive or negative), we are observing it and causing it to collapse into form. The results show up in the circumstances of our lives.

So, I ask you, to what are you paying attention? Does what you watch on TV or what you read uplift you? Does that input leave you with a good feeling? How about the people you associate with on a daily basis? Are they positive, or are you subjected to gossip and complaining? Remember that your five senses are processing input all day, every day. Awareness is a good thing. If your focus was on what's right in the world, you would be collapsing into form more goodness. If you're one who frets on the problems and terror in the world, then guess what? It's probably a good thing to be aware of your current events, but it's another thing to harbor the ugliness you hear about or see. Your mind is a creative machine.

We are seeing a heck of a lot of more negative things going on in today's world than we'd like to see, and it's scary for sure. We actually have to dig to look for the good stuff. I encourage you to do just that, because you can easily get sucked into the negativity, and you will bring it right into your own world. As one person, we can't change the world itself to any great degree, but our responsibility is to change our own world and teach others to do the same, even if it's just by our example. Believe it or not, that does have a multiplying effect. Simply do your job, and let the universe handle the rest.

You can start right now, with the awareness you've gained in just these pages. Smile, look for things to be grateful for, enjoy the good food you're eating, and say hello to someone. Congratulate yourself with each simple change. Know that as your attitude changes, you are collapsing into form the life that's calling to you, as well as the happiness you deserve. Start at the quantum level!

You are a powerful creator. With the entire universe, as creative potential, consciously focus on that which is good about your life, knowing that more of this good is on the way to you. Starting small can bring the biggest results.

SECTION 8

An Ending and a Beginning

Considering the real age of this planet, the history of the civilized thinking man is relatively short. Man's curiosity about what's out there in the early times was focused primarily on the physical. Take Christopher Columbus, for example. He set off from Spain to not only discover new lands beyond what he knew, but to disprove the theory that the world was flat and that he'd sail so far and fall off the edge somewhere. His inspirations proved true because he did discover new territories in the beyond, and he didn't fall off at the end of the horizon. He was one of many who left the old and started a new beginning. Therefore, aren't we bountifully blessed to have a new beginning each day we open our eyes?

We have a round planet, as you know, and as a sphere, every seeming end is a beginning of something else. Let's expand on this a bit. You've heard the term "cycle of life," I'm sure. Most would explain that it's the process of human life from birth to death. Well, take into consideration what I've shared with you here about the life process, and the fact that we are actually spiritual beings having human experiences. Do you believe that this cycle—which is also a circle, I might add—begins at physical birth and ends at physical death? In one aspect, yes. But can you grasp the concept that there is no finality and that the real self is immortal? Also, I might add that all the knowledge and awareness that you've amassed in this lifetime has raised you to a being of higher understanding, and it becomes locked in as a part of your soul-self and follows you endlessly. I could go on here, but that could be material for another sharing down the road, and I think you get the picture. The point I'm driving at is that there is an inborn desire within us, whether or not we are conscious of it, to better ourselves and grow and to express ourselves. Once aware, we can't be unaware. Beginning again always happens.

However, you are here now, and I hope what you've taken the time to read here has brought you to either a deeper awareness of self, or at the very least got you thinking in the realm of what-if. As I alluded to in the beginning, widen the perspective on the life you are living, as well as that marvelous being looking back at you from the mirror.

Perspective is important because you are considering making changes in your current situation. I remember when I was sharing such ideas with clients. I would ask them to close their eyes and pretend that they were standing in front of their house. I asked them to describe to me what it looked like. Then I'd have them take me on a tour inside the home and let them describe the inside as well. Most could do a pretty good job of that (as you could, I'm sure). Next, I had them go up on the roof and tell me what they could see from there. With that expanded view, they could see so much more of what their home was a part of. The idea was that the higher your awareness, the farther you can see, and the smaller some problems could now be.

How far can you see? I know you can see where you came from, but I'm asking if you can see your future. I'm asking if you can see who you really are. Allow me to tell you who you really are: you are a creator-being and a child of light!

It is unfortunate that so many people feel that they don't have the power to make major changes in their own lives—and for that reason, they could not possibly be creating their own reality. What they don't realize is that their thoughts, feelings, and beliefs simply provide the energy to send a signal out into the universe. It is the universe that amplifies this signal by adding all the energy required to rearrange a personal reality and manifest a new life experience.

If people knew that they have the power to ask the universe to change their reality, then they would understand that they are not weak and helpless victims of circumstances, but are empowered children of the light exercising their birthright as creator-beings. A being of light is empowered to ask the universe because the universe is itself made of light. In a sense, when you send a signal out in the universe, you are sending a signal into the essence of your own being. It is because the universe recognizes you as a child of light, as being one with itself in essence, that it obeys your request. Thus, manifesting a reality is fundamentally you and the universe being as one and moving as one. This is the real secret of your own nature and your own power.

Go forth, knowing that tomorrow is the most important day of your life. Your greatest moment, your greatest adventure, your greatest achievement lies in the future, never in the past. There is a new you waiting to be created tomorrow. Forget about yesterday! What is the grandest version of the greatest vision you held about who you are going to be tomorrow? That is the only question that matters.

Liberty isn't just a concept. It is the carefree feeling of mastery that comes from knowing we create our own reality. Take the liberty to choose for your highest good.

Every man's life is a plan of God. You are here to lead a full, happy, and glorious life. You are here to release your hidden talents to the world, to find your true place in life, and to express yourself at your highest level.

SECTION 9

New Lifestyle

Introducing and making major changes in our lives takes commitment, faith, perseverance, and self-love. It is not the easiest task we'll ever take on. We don't like change. In fact, most of us fear it and try to hide from it. It is a constant of life in one form or another. The only thing that doesn't change is change itself. I understand all this because I've seen it in working with others over the years and in myself. Sometimes I'm my own worst enemy, and I've tried to deny change in order to stay in a comfort zone I've created. Doing this has certainly denied my growth, because life is all about growth. It's been a long road and sometimes a hard road, however, and I am blessed. For me, this book has been an important part of my calling to serve and, at the same time, grow by stepping out from my comfort zone. I did my best to allow the message within me to come out for you. This has changed me and changed my life, just like it has done in the past when I stepped out beyond, leaving an old and unfulfilled part of myself behind to express what was in my heart. Simply knowing I needed to help people in a dutiful way signaled the universe to open avenues for me to pursue it. The original hunger is still there, but the avenues to feed it are seemingly a little different. They're exciting because I know there are still more old parts of me to be left behind with gratitude.

To be honest, taking on the task of bringing change of any degree to your life is very serious business. You must be prepared to rock your whole state of being. What I've presented here is a behind-the-scenes, under-the-iceberg look at the process of bringing something from your thoughts to your third-dimensional reality. You need to be aware of these things as you step on the pathway to true ownership of every aspect of your life. Making conscious choices and expecting them to show up is a natural, God-given right. It promotes a shift in consciousness that literally realigns your lifestyle. I know it sounds scary, but using this awareness and allowing the universe to do what it does is like being driven to a destination by a chauffeur. You're getting where you want to go without having to deal with the traffic.

There are so many benefits to a lifestyle that exudes meaning and purpose. You notice a difference in every aspect of your demeanor and even your personality. You will now exercise your freedom, because bondage is not God-ordained and freedom is the expression of your soul. You will attract success as you realize that there is no failure, only results. You pursue happiness as you choose joy in every moment. You become empowered as you begin to re-create yourself from the inside out. You honor your soul by listening to your heart rather than the ego in your head. You dream big because you know that you deserve it and nothing can keep you from it. You actually embrace change just because it's exciting to see what's around the corner. Surprisingly, you eliminate worry because you are at peace with your world and now know that worry is a function of the untrained mind. You forgive frequently, starting with yourself, because when you forgive, you are free. You notice you are prone to random acts of kindness because these very acts boomerang back to you at some point. You laugh more, as laughter is the song of the happy, free soul. And most important, you guard your thoughts because you now know that what you think about expands. Remember what Theodore Roosevelt once said, "If you could kick the person in the pants responsible for most of your trouble, you wouldn't sit for a month."

These are just a few of the lifestyle changes that are awaiting you when you step out and take back control, follow your dreams and passions. and become one with the very Source that brought you here and yearns to express that life through you. Find some of your own benefits. Don't be afraid. Start small if you must, but start. Live life! Take a step forward toward your greatest fulfillment and live a life of joy. A co-creator is what you are. Batteries and instructions are included. Once we have secured our connection with the divinity within us, we are meant to go out and do great things!

SECTION 10

Simplicity, Inspiration, and Empowerment

My dear reader, at this closing juncture, herein lies your bottom line. Everything—and I do mean everything—is already created! It is the greatest unknown, and thus the unutilized truth of which we need to be aware. Being unaware of that truth is the very reason we want and desire in the first place, because all we're seeing is that the want or desire doesn't now exist in our individual realities.

We've come to understand that each of us is a part of the one Source, God. We are complete with all that God is composed of. Like an eyedropper full of ocean water, each drop has within it all that the ocean itself has. Each is an ocean unto itself, if you will. We have what God is!

You may ask, "What is our part, exactly?" Simply put, through our desire for something that we don't think we have but would like to experience, we are calling infinite universal substance into form in our individual realities. At this point, we become open to inspiration from the universal mind that stimulates our imagination. That creative imagination joins hands with this personal desire by way of developing an attitude of already having received. Once we've perceived that we've received, the accompanying emotions go to work to bring that imagined reality into form in your physical space. At that point, you are empowered.

Sounds simple, right? If I could only see your face as your wheels are spinning. This simplified version of manifesting in no way excludes the fact I brought to bear earlier, in that you must certainly be a clear vessel. Here's what I suggest right now while thoughts are whirling around in your head. Reach out for inspiration, an inner whisper from that voiceless voice within that can make your heart jump. Seek it from the world with which you coexist. It's everywhere, from the majesty of nature to the lowly panhandlers on the street corners of your own town. It's all God, talking to you in some fashion, giving you hints and pointing out ideas and directions to take on your walk of life. Read more material on this subject. Listen to wisdom from many sources. Let the material touch you in whatever way it can, in order to help you become aware of what you are, why you are here, and what you have to do or be. Become empowered enough to do the work and reap the life-changing benefits.

As you bathe yourself in inspiration, it is like the sprinkling of seeds on fertile soil. As they sit on this fertile ground, they come in contact with the nutrients of the soil. When it's time, they begin to germinate and become what it is to become. This whole book may be something like that for you. I can only hope. Deep truth delivered from inspiration requires time to germinate within the receiver. We need to sit with it. Some seeds may take longer to unfold their hidden radiance, if not now, then when the time is right. Be assured that there is a time for you. Make no mistake about that. You simply wouldn't be here if that wasn't true. Look to celebrate yourself and your life.

In a nutshell my friends, co-creating or manifesting, be it by intension or even by default, is best explained by this example. Imagine that what you want, (or don't want) has already come into fruition. You are living your life from that mindset. You predicate your behavior on that reality rather than the illusions that now surround you. You filter every thought, question and answer from there. This shifts your focus and you are "born again", because you are now dwelling from, not upon the space you want, (or don't want) to inherit which is the fastest way to change absolutely everything.

For proper co-creation one needs to be in the scene experiencing the end result. To create a new reality, you create an event that exists in your future, not in your present. When you are in that scene witnessing the end result of your desired reality, you are operating in your imagination at some point in the future.

Becoming empowered is like making it up to the top of a mountain. The air is clearer, and you can see for miles. You get a feeling that it's all good, and you are at peace with everything as it is and with everyone, no matter how they present themselves. You know and accept that they have their roads as you have yours, and just as you've driven your car to the top, so must they by whatever routes they are guided.

Thank you for allowing me to share my passion with you. I welcome your comments (good, bad, or indifferent) and questions. Feel free to contact me anytime at <u>Drronsgenesis101@gmail.com</u>.

ABOUT THE AUTHOR

Ronald Rozzi, MsD, RHy, holds a doctorate in metaphysics and is certified in both hypnotherapy and regression therapy. He is also a practitioner of emotional freedom therapy (EFT). He specialized in past-life regression and anxiety disorder, as well as behavioral modification. He is currently semiretired from his private practice of eighteen years. He doesn't really believe one can ever fully retire from helping people learn and heal. He enjoys speaking to groups, as well as now writing. At this stage of life, he feels it's vital to educate and empower through awareness. His passion now centers around the depths of self and the connection with universal law.

In a completely different light, Dr. Rozzi's second passion, which first started at age ten, is the American Civil War. He considers himself an armchair historian on the subject and specializes in the Battle of Gettysburg. He visits there and walks the fields at least twice a year. He and his wife reside in Scottsville, New York. He can be contacted via e-mail anytime at Drronsgenesis101@gmail.com.

CERTIFICATIONS

Certified Hypnotherapist
 The Hypnosis Learning Institute, Clearwater Florida, 07/16/1994
 International Association of Counselors and Therapists, 07/16/1994

Doctor of Metaphysics
 The College of Divine Metaphysics, Glendora California, 03/07/1995

Past Life Regression Therapist
 Henry L. Bolduc CH, Henry Reed PhD, Wytheville, VA, 10/23/1999

Certified Past Life Regression Therapist
 American Alliance of Hypnotists, Dr. Steve G. Jones, Savanah, GA, 10/10/16

Certified Advanced Past Life Regression Therapist
 American Alliance of Hypnotists, Dr. Steve G. Jones, Savanah, GA 11/17/16

Certified Hypnosis Instructor
   Hypnosis International Board of Registration, Clearwater FL
   Hypnodyne Foundation 06/19/2000

Emotional Freedom Therapy Practitioner 02/26/2007
   Gary Craig, Founder, EFT

ACKNOWLEDGMENTS

The path to this, my first book, was paved with the lives and experiences of the many beautiful people who came to me over the years and shared so much of their stories, trials, tears, and hopes. Through them, I learned much about life and death in the physical and was able to hone my skills relative to the metaphysical in order to help them see a larger and different perspective. It was not so much to minimize their pain as to use it as a springboard to a better, more productive and fulfilling life. I remain thankful and blessed to have been allowed in to some very private, personal spaces and trusted to give them tools and concepts to grow.

Of course, in the time it took me to write this book, there are two people who pushed me the most. One is my wonderful wife, Mary Lou. Without her undying love and support, this work may still be sitting on my shelf, unfinished. She always knew that finishing this was a part of me that was missing, and she wanted all of me as her husband. My eternal love and thanks to you, princess.

The other is my good friend James McDowell. This gentle, good man has been a continued support from the beginning. Nearly every day, when I'd see him, he'd always ask, "How's the book coming, Ron? You've got to get that done!" His smile and laugh never leave me, and his friendship is genuine. Thanks, Jimmy!

RESOURCES

The NIV Bible, Tyndale House Publishers, Carol Stream IL., Book of Genesis (1:1–2:3)

Holmes, Earnest, *The Science of Mind*, G.P. Putnam's Sons, NY., NY 1966

Holmes, Earnest, *Creative Mind and Success*, G.P. Putnam's Sons, NY., NY 1957

Holmes, Earnest, *This Thing Called Life*, G.P. Putnam's Sons, NY., NY 1943

Holmes, Earnest, *This Thing Called You*, G.P. Putnam's Sons NY., NY 1948

Science of Mind Guide for Spiritual Living, Science of Mind Publications, Golden Colorado, April 2011, August 2011, February 2011, April 2016, August 2016

Clark, Glenn, *The Man Who Tapped the Secrets of the Universe*, University of Science and Philosophy, Waynesboro Va., 1946

Murphy, Joseph, *How to Use the Laws of Mind*, DeVorss & Company, Marina Del Rey, CA., 1980

McArthur, Bruce, *Your Life, Understanding the Universal Laws*, A.R.E. Press, Virginia Beach, VA., 1993

Fersen, Eugene, *Science of Being*, Ultimate Reality Publications, 2008

Newton, Michael, *Journey of Souls*, Llewellyn Publications, St. Paul MN., 1995

Chilton, Pamela, *Odyssey of the Soul*, Quick Book Publishing, Rancho Mirage CA., 1997

Walsch, Neal Donald, *Recreating Your Self*, Millennium Legacies Inc., Ashland, OR., 1995

Walsch, Neal Donald, *Bringers of the Light*, Millennium Legacies Inc., Ashland, OR., 1995

Dooley, Michael, *Infinite Possibilities*, Beyond Words Publishing, NY. NY., 2009

Waters, Owen, *The Shift*, Infinite Being Publishing LLc., Delaware, 2006

Atkinson, William, *Thought Vibration*, Nightingale Conant, Chicago IL., 1983

Moss, Louie, *68 Seconds to Becoming Wealthy*, Higher Ground Holdings, 2002

Tan, Enoch, *The Secrets of Mind Reality*, Mind Reality Publications, Singapore

www.ingramcontent.com/pod-product-compliance
Lightning Source LLC
Chambersburg PA
CBHW052107070526
44584CB00017B/2379